Animal H

Written by Margie Burton, Cathy Fr

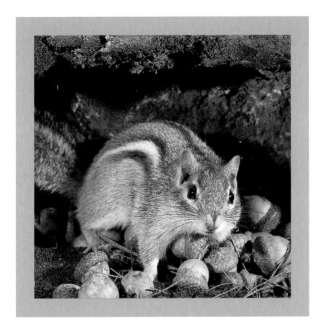

The bird is in a home.

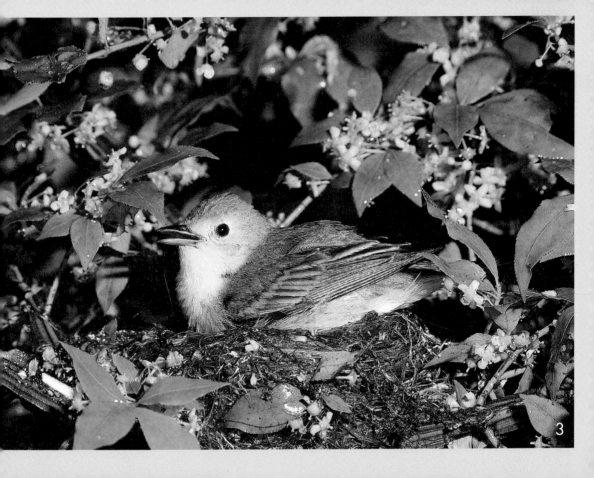

3

The dog is in a home.

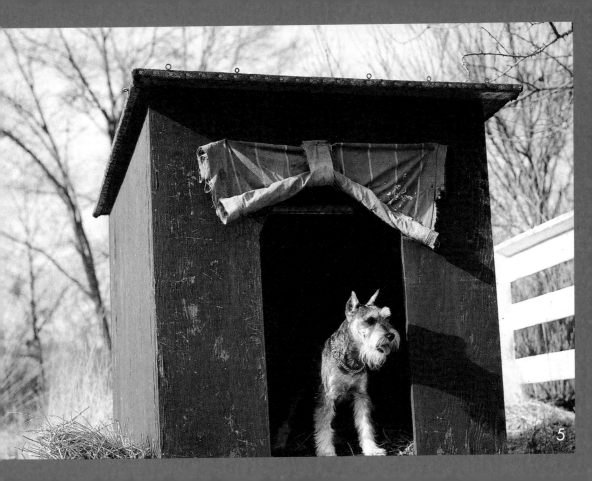

The bee is in
a home.

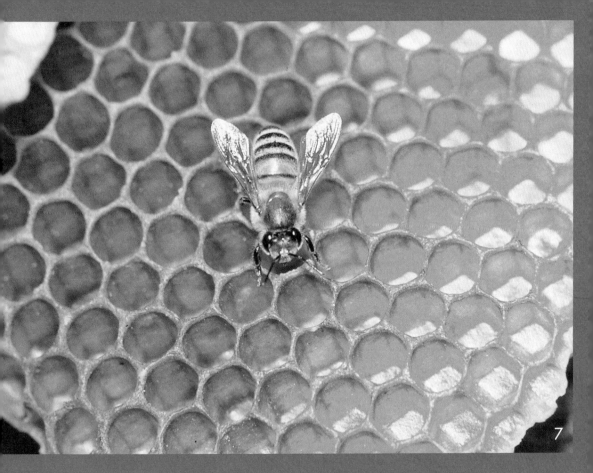

The pig is in
a home.

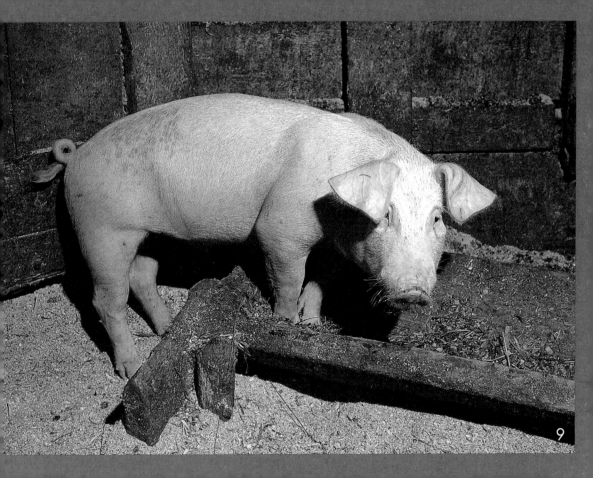

The turtle is in
a home.

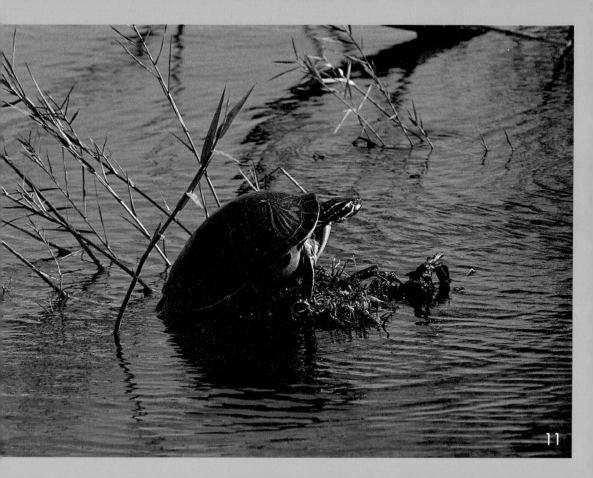

The snake is in
a home.

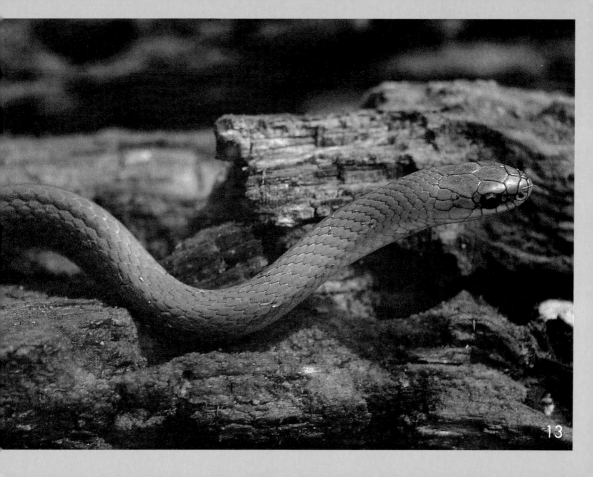

The fish is in a home.

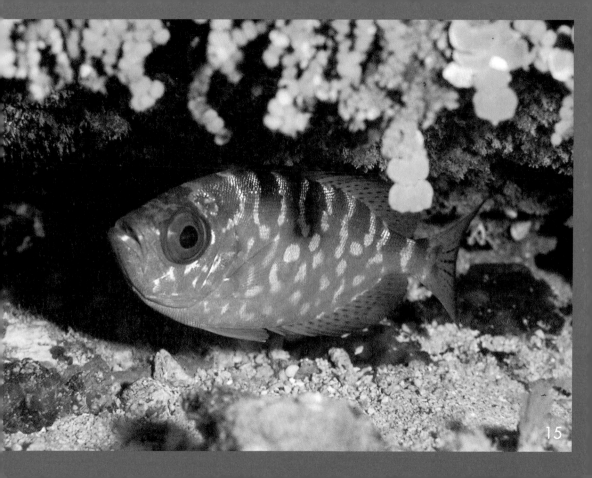

Is the tiger in a home?

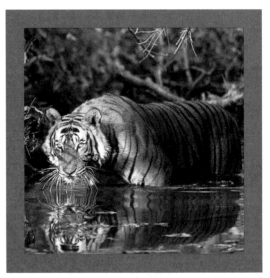